ARMADILLO

By Jenna Grodzicki

Consultant: Darin Collins, DVM
Director, Animal Health Programs, Woodland Park Zoo

BEARPORT
PUBLISHING

Minneapolis, Minnesota

Credits

Cover and title page, © Colin Pickett/Alamy, © Gala__Kan/iStock; 3, © Alicia Ramirez/Shutterstock; 4–5, © agefotostock/Alamy; 7, © klausbalzano/iStock; 8, © MH STOCK/Shutterstock; 9, © Science History Images/Alamy; 11, © Foto 4440/Shutterstock; 12, © BERNATSKAIA OKSANA/Shutterstock; 13, © James Davies/Alamy; 15, © Nature Picture Library/Alamy; 16–17, © Heidi and Hans-Juergen Koch/Minden; 19, © Rose Waddell/Shutterstock; 20, © moose henderson/iStock; 21, © Ondrej Prosicky/iStock; 23, © Marcelo Morena/Shutterstock

President: Jen Jenson
Director of Product Development: Spencer Brinker
Senior Editor: Allison Juda
Associate Editor: Charly Haley
Designer: Colin O'Dea

Library of Congress Cataloging-in-Publication Data

Names: Grodzicki, Jenna, 1979- author.
Title: Armadillo / by Jenna Grodzicki.
Description: Minneapolis, Minnesota : Bearport Publishing Company, [2022] | Series: Library of awesome animals | Includes bibliographical references and index.
Identifiers: LCCN 2020057392 (print) | LCCN 2020057393 (ebook) | ISBN 9781636911458 (library binding) | ISBN 9781636911533 (paperback) | ISBN 9781636911618 (ebook)
Subjects: LCSH: Armadillos--Juvenile literature.
Classification: LCC QL737.E23 G76 2022 (print) | LCC QL737.E23 (ebook) | DDC 599.3/12--dc23
LC record available at https://lccn.loc.gov/2020057392
LC ebook record available at https://lccn.loc.gov/2020057393

For more information, write to Bearport Publishing, 5357 Penn Avenue South, Minneapolis, MN 55419. Printed in the United States of America.

Contents

Awesome Armadillos! 4

A Mammal in Shining Armor 6

I'm with the Bands 8

Home Sweet Home 10

Tasty Treats 12

Look Out! 14

Here Come the Pups 16

Mom's in Charge. 18

Growing Up 20

Information Station 22
Glossary 23
Index 24
Read More 24
Learn More Online. 24
About the Author. 24

AWESOME
Armadillos!

SNIFF, SNIFF! An armadillo scurries along with its **snout** on the ground. Sniffing out snacks or slurping up bugs with sticky tongues, armadillos are awesome!

ARMADILLOS CAN SMELL FOOD AS DEEP AS 8 INCHES (20 CM) BELOW THE GROUND.

A Mammal in Shining Armor

The armadillo is the only **mammal** with a shell. Its **armor** is made of bony plates covered by thick, hard skin. This protects the animal's soft back, legs, head, and tail. But the skin under the armor is stretchy, which lets the armadillo move the different hard pieces, called bands, as it needs to.

THE NAME *ARMADILLO* COMES FROM A SPANISH WORD MEANING LITTLE ARMORED ONE.

An armadillo band

I'm with the Bands

There are many kinds of armadillos. Some are named after the number of bands they have. Three-banded armadillos have three bands of armor. Six-banded armadillos have (can you guess?) six bands.

A three-banded armadillo

A six-banded armadillo

Long hair hangs from armadillos' undersides. The hair and armored bands can come in many colors, including brown, black, red, gray, or yellow.

THE SMALL PINK FAIRY ARMADILLO HAS PINK ARMOR AND WHITE HAIR.

A pink fairy armadillo

Home Sweet Home

The nine-banded armadillo is the only kind that lives in the United States. All other armadillos live in Central and South America. Armadillos make their homes in warm places with loose, sandy **soil**. They use their powerful claws to dig **burrows** where they often live alone and spend up to 16 hours a day sleeping.

ARMADILLOS ARE MOSTLY NOCTURNAL. THEY ARE ACTIVE AT NIGHT.

Tasty Treats

When armadillos finally wake up, they spend their time searching for food and eating. They can't see very well, so they rely on their strong sense of smell. Once they sniff out their meal, they dig it up with those powerful claws. *GULP!* Bugs are at the top of the menu, but armadillos also eat plants, fruits, and small dead animals.

ARMADILLOS GRUNT LIKE PIGS WHILE SEARCHING FOR FOOD.

Look Out!

Armadillos move slowly when looking for food, but they can run fast if they're in danger of becoming the meal. *ZOOM!* Armadillos will scurry back to their burrows to hide from **predators**, including coyotes, bobcats, dogs, and alligators.

Humans are also a **threat** to armadillos. Some people eat armadillos. The animals also face **habitat** loss as humans clear away their land.

THE THREE-BANDED ARMADILLO CAN CURL INTO A BALL TO PROTECT ITSELF FROM PREDATORS.

Here Come the Pups

In the summer, armadillos come together to **mate**. Many kinds of armadillos have one to three babies at a time. But some have been known to give birth to more than 10 babies at once. Baby armadillos are called pups. They look like mini adults!

NINE-BANDED ARMADILLOS ALWAYS GIVE BIRTH TO FOUR IDENTICAL BABIES AT A TIME.

Mom's in Charge

Armadillo pups are born with soft shells. To stay safe, the babies stay in their burrow with their mother for the first few weeks. They drink milk from her body and grow. After three or four weeks, the pups follow their mother outside. Then, the young armadillos learn how to find food on their own. As they get older, their shells harden.

ARMADILLO PUPS CAN WALK WHEN THEY ARE JUST A FEW HOURS OLD.

Growing Up

Armadillo pups stay with their mothers until they are about six months old. Then, it's time for them to head out into the world. **SEE YA!** By the time they reach their first birthday, most armadillos are ready to have their own babies.

IN THE WILD, ARMADILLOS CAN LIVE ANYWHERE FROM 4 TO 30 YEARS.

ARMADILLOS ARE AWESOME!
LET'S LEARN EVEN MORE ABOUT THEM.

Kind of animal: Armadillos are mammals. Most mammals have fur, give birth to live young, and drink milk from their mothers as babies.

More armadillos: There are 20 different types of armadillos.

Size: Different armadillos are different sizes. The smallest armadillo is only about 6 in. (15 cm) long. That is about the size of a chipmunk.

ARMADILLOS AROUND THE WORLD

Arctic Ocean

NORTH AMERICA

EUROPE

ASIA

Pacific Ocean

Atlantic Ocean

AFRICA

Pacific Ocean

SOUTH AMERICA

Indian Ocean

N
W E
S

AUSTRALIA

Southern Ocean

ANTARCTICA

WHERE ARMADILLOS LIVE

Glossary

armor a hard covering that protects the body

burrows holes or tunnels in the ground where animals live

habitat a place in nature where an animal lives

identical similar in every way

mammal an animal that has fur, gives birth to live young, and drinks milk from its mother's body as a baby

mate to come together to have young

nocturnal active at night

predators animals that hunt and kill other animals for food

snout the long nose of some animals

soil the top layer of the earth's surface

Index

armor 6, 8–9
bands 6–9, 14
burrow 10, 14, 18
claws 10, 12
habitat 15
hair 8–9
insects 12

mammals 6, 22
mate 16
predators 14
pups 16, 18, 20
snout 4
soil 10
tongue 4

Read More

Knopf, Susan. *Armadillos: Dynamite Diggers (Nature's Children).* New York: Children's Press, 2020.

Riggs, Kate. *Armadillos (Amazing Animals).* Mankato, MN: Creative Education, 2018.

Learn More Online

1. Go to **www.factsurfer.com**
2. Enter "**Armadillo**" into the search box.
3. Click on the cover of this book to see a list of websites.

About the Author

Jenna Grodzicki lives on beautiful Cape Cod with her husband and two children. She was a teacher for a long time before she became a writer. She loves to read and go to the beach.